OCT   2005

GREAT MOMENTS IN
FOOTBALL

by James Buckley Jr.

WORLD ALMANAC® LIBRARY

Please visit our web site at: www.worldalmanaclibrary.com
For a free color catalog describing World Almanac® Library's
list of high-quality books and multimedia programs,
call 1-800-848-2928 (USA) or 1-800-387-3178 (Canada).
World Almanac® Library's fax: (414) 332-3567.

Library of Congress Cataloging-in-Publication Data

Buckley, James, Jr.
    Great moments in football / by James Buckley, Jr. — North American ed.
       p. cm. — (Great moments in sports)
    Summary: Recounts ten high points in the history of football, including the first NFL
Championship game to be televised, the "Immaculate Reception" by Franco Harris in
1972, and the comeback by the Buffalo Bills in the 1993 AFC playoff game.
    Includes bibliographical references and index.
    ISBN 0-8368-5346-6 (lib. bdg.)
    ISBN 0-8368-5360-1 (softcover)
    1. Football—United States—History—Juvenile literature. [1. Football—History.] I. Title.
II. Great moments in sports (Milwaukee, Wis.)
GV950.7.B84   2002
796.332'0973—dc21   2002016855

This North American edition first published in 2002 by
World Almanac® Library
330 West Olive Street, Suite 100
Milwaukee, WI 53212 USA

This U.S. edition © 2002 by World Almanac® Library.

An Editorial Directions book
Editor: Lucia Raatma
Photo researcher: Image Select International Ltd.
Copy editor: Melissa McDaniel
Proofreader: Sarah De Capua
Indexer: Tim Griffin
Art direction, design, and page production: The Design Lab
World Almanac® Library editorial direction: Mark J. Sachner
World Almanac® Library art direction: Tammy Gruenewald
World Almanac® Library production: Susan Ashley and Jessica L. Yanke

Photographs ©: Getty Images, cover; Corbis, 3, 5; Getty Images, 6, 7, 8; Corbis, 9; Getty
Images, 10; Corbis, 11, 12; Getty Images 13; Corbis, 14; Getty Images, 15; Corbis, 16, 17;
Getty Images, 18; Corbis, 19, 20, 21; Getty Images, 22; Corbis, 23, 24; Getty Images, 25;
Corbis, 26; Copyright 1982 by Robert B. Stinnett, 28 top; Getty Images, 28 bottom;
Corbis, 29, 30, 31, 32; Getty Images 33, 34, 36, 37 left; 37 right, 38, 39, 40, 41; Reuters/
Popperfoto, 42; AFP, 44; Reuters/Popperfoto, 45 top; AFP, 45 bottom.

Opposite: *San Francisco 49ers wide receiver
Jerry Rice (80), shown here running the
ball against the Atlanta Falcons, holds an
incredible array of career and single-season
NFL receiving records. In Super Bowl XXIII,
Rice won the game MVP award as the 49ers
scored a dramatic comeback win over the
Cincinnati Bengals.*

Contents

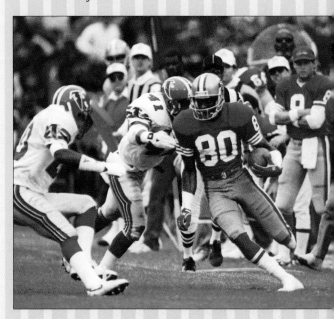

Introduction

If you look at the numbers, football is America's most popular sport. More than 100 million people watch National Football League (NFL) games on TV every Sunday in the fall, with another 19 million or so attending in person over the course of a season. Tens of millions of people watch college football games on TV and in person. Every town in America has at least one high school football team that draws a big crowd. Plus, the Super Bowl is the single highest-rated television program nearly every year. Sometimes as many at 130 million Americans watch it, and an estimated 500 million more watch broadcasts of the game around the world in more than a dozen languages.

By nearly every measure of popularity, football is number one. Through the years, football, both professional and college, has given fans hundreds of great moments to remember. Incredible touchdown runs, heart-stopping

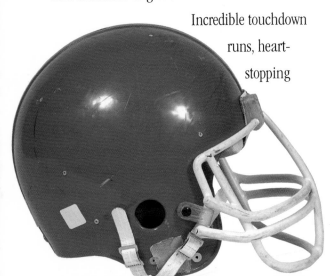

finishes, miracle comebacks, heroes large and small, battles against the elements, all have been seen on gridirons from Florida to Fargo and everywhere in between—and even lots of places beyond that!

What is it about football that breeds such glorious moments? One reason is the format of the game itself. A game occurs in four quarters that are almost like chapters in a book, with each chapter adding more and more to the story until, at the end, the final score reveals the ending to the tale. But anything can happen in those quarters. A team that should be smashed somehow comes out on top. A bouncing ball can end up in the right hands and suddenly turn a game, a season, and a team around.

Another reason can be summed up in a famous statement often used to describe the beauty of NFL football. "On any given Sunday," the saying goes, "any team can beat any other team." In other words, when that referee's whistle blows and the ball is kicked off, you just never really know what is going to happen.

Sometimes what happens are moments for the ages, the work of men whose lives and deeds are celebrated as the greatest in all of sports, men like Jim Thorpe and Joe Montana. Sometimes the moments are pure fantasy, a weird mix of the

Lambeau Field, home of the Green Bay Packers and the site of one of football's most exciting play-off games ever—the "Ice Bowl" between Green Bay and Dallas on New Year's Eve, 1967. The "frozen tundra" of Lambeau has given Green Bay one of the most remarkable home-field advantages in sports history; the Pack has never lost a play-off game at this storied stadium.

bizarre and the amazing, all played out in front of the eyes of fans in the stands and on TV, such as the improbable plays in Pittsburgh and Berkeley described in this book. And sometimes the moments are ones of triumph, of championship, of a team rising above all obstacles to win, no matter what the odds.

For more than a hundred years, football players and teams have been making such moments happen. This book celebrates ten of the greatest events that have stood the test of time and stand out above others in the fans' collective memory. You might not find what you call the "greatest" football moment in here; that's okay, you can tell your own "greatest" story to your friends just as well as the stories are told in this book.

Because a football moment, no matter how great or how ordinary, will live on forever as long as someone tells the tale.

WA-THO-HUCK, ALL-AMERICAN

Jim Thorpe Becomes Football's First Superstar

On November 11, 1911 (that's right—11/11/11), more than 30,000 people filled Harvard Stadium in Cambridge, Massachusetts. The powerful Harvard University football team had invited the tiny Carlisle Indian School to Cambridge to play, thinking that they could get in an easy game during the middle of the season. Thanks to Jim Thorpe, Harvard was wrong.

Jim Thorpe will long be remembered as a great football player and a truly remarkable all-around athlete.

The Harvard-Carlisle matchup didn't seem fair on paper. Carlisle was good but had few of the advantages that rich and powerful Harvard had. Plus, Harvard hadn't lost during the 1910 season. (In fact, it wouldn't lose in 1912, 1913, or 1914 either; the school started a thirty-three-game winning streak the week after playing Carlisle.)

A Secret Weapon

Carlisle, located in Pennsylvania, was one of several small colleges dedicated to educating Native Americans. (Though the purpose of these schools was education, they were also used to turn Native Americans away from their own culture and toward that of white Americans.) Like other "Indian schools," Carlisle was not known for having blockbuster sports teams. But Carlisle had one secret weapon. Its team boasted a young member of the Sac and Fox tribe who had made a great name for himself in track and field and baseball. To his family, he was Wa-Tho-Huck, or "Bright Path." But to the sports world, he was Jim Thorpe, one of the most amazing athletes of all time.

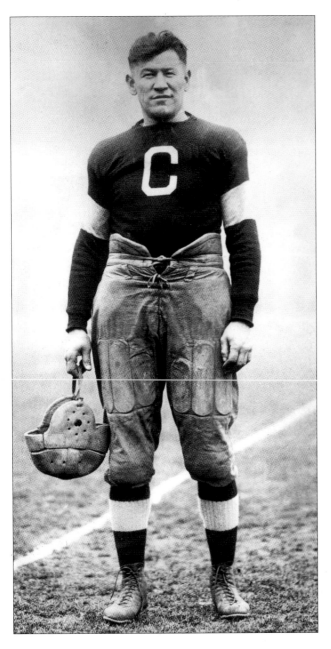

Led by Thorpe, shown here in his Carlisle Indian School football uniform, Carlisle captured the national college football championship in 1912.

Like all football players in those days, Thorpe played on both offense (as a running back) and defense (as a hard-hitting linebacker). (They often played without helmets, and few players wore any protective gear beyond thick

DROP THAT KICK!

Thorpe excelled at a special kind of kick not seen in football today. Today, a field-goal kicker kicks the ball from a spot on the field where it is held upright by a teammate. In Thorpe's day, kickers used the "drop-kick."

The kicker took a couple of steps, then dropped the ball straight down in front of him. The instant the ball bounced back up from the ground, the player swung his leg and struck the football with the toe of his football shoe, sending the ball toward the goalpost.

Back then, footballs were rounder and less pointy, so a ball dropped straight down usually bounced back up in the same direction. Thorpe was amazingly accurate from long range. On a visit to a field when he was fifty-two years old, he drop-kicked a pair of 50-yard (45.7-meter) field goals . . . while wearing street shoes!

The drop-kick is still legal today, but the sharper shape of the ball means that it is nearly impossible to drop-kick accurately.

Jim Thorpe preparing to throw the discus at the 1912 Olympic Games in Stockholm, Sweden, where he won gold medals in the pentathlon and decathlon.

canvas pants.) Thorpe was also the team's kicker and punter, and his four field goals proved to be the difference in the game against Harvard. Almost single-handedly, Thorpe knocked off the mighty Harvard Crimson team and put Carlisle Indian School on the national sports map, as the little school from Pennsylvania won 18–15.

Carlisle would go on to lose only one game all season, and Thorpe became the first Native American athlete ever named to the All-America football team. He repeated that feat in 1912, scoring twenty-five touchdowns. Adding in his field goals and extra-point kicks, he had a total of 198 points on the season. That year,

Carlisle again faced some of the nation's top schools, such as Brown, Army, and Pittsburgh, and, led by Thorpe, emerged as the national college football champions. It was one of the smallest schools ever to capture this honor.

A Legendary Athlete

While Thorpe's legend as a football player grew out of his Carlisle exploits, his story as an athlete was just beginning. The next summer, he traveled to Stockholm, Sweden, for the 1912 Summer Olympics, where he became the only athlete ever to win the pentathlon (a competition of five track-and-field events) and the decathlon (ten events) in the same Olympics. (Sadly, a short stint playing minor-league baseball led Olympic officials to strip Thorpe of his amateur status and take back his two gold medals in 1913. They were returned, however, in 1984, thirty-one years after his death.)

At the Olympics, the king of Sweden had called Thorpe "the greatest athlete in the world." Thorpe was certainly one of the most versatile. Along with his track success, he starred in lacrosse and basketball at Carlisle, was a professional baseball player with the New York Giants, and played pro football for twelve seasons. He also was a skilled golfer, and he once even won a ballroom-dancing competition!

For two seasons, Thorpe was the greatest college football player of his era, but that was just the first step on his road to sports immortality.

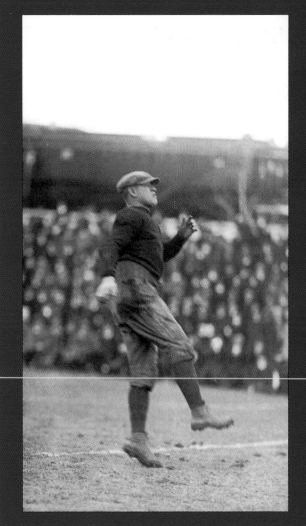

GOIN' PRO

Thorpe's final college football season was 1912, but that wasn't the end of his football career. In 1915, he joined a pro team, the Canton Bulldogs, and helped them win three championships. In 1920, he was named as the president of a new professional league that two years later would become today's National Football League. He continued playing until 1926, starring for several teams, including the short-lived Oorang Indians, a team he formed using all Native American players.

In 1963, Thorpe was named as one of the charter members of the Pro Football Hall of Fame.

"THE GREATEST GAME EVER PLAYED"

The NFL's Popularity Booms in 1958

Thanks to one incredible, heart-stopping, nail-biting game, the National Football League turned from a second-rank league into the juggernaut that dominates sports in America today. In the 1950s, professional football trailed baseball, college football, and perhaps even boxing on the list of America's favorite sports. But a fairly new invention called television was helping more and more people see the drama, action, and speed of the NFL, and that invention would give the NFL its biggest boost yet on December 28, 1958.

That day, for the first time, the NFL championship game was televised nationwide. Not everyone had a TV in those days, but the medium had spread far and wide enough that millions of viewers around the country could tune in to watch the New York Giants take on the Baltimore Colts in front of more than 67,000 people in New York's Yankee Stadium (usually the home of baseball's Yankees).

Baltimore Colts great Johnny Unitas led his team to a sudden-death overtime victory over the New York Giants for the 1958 NFL Championship.

Battling to a Tie

The first quarter of the game was slow, with the Giants managing only a field goal. In the second quarter, the Colts turned two fumbles by New York's Frank Gifford into touchdowns to take a 14–3 halftime lead. The stadium full of Giants fans began to worry about their heroes.

New York's fortunes changed in the second half. After Colts quarterback Johnny Unitas marched Baltimore to the Giants' five-yard line, the New York defense held and the Colts didn't score. A few plays later, Giants quarterback Charlie Conerly hit Kyle Rote with a 62-yard (57-m) pass. Rote fumbled as he was tackled, but teammate Alex Webster recovered and ran to the 1-yard line, from where Mel Triplett scored soon after.

In the fourth quarter, Gifford caught a

This 1958 overtime game was the first important NFL game decided in extra time, but it was not the only one. On Christmas Day, 1971, the Miami Dolphins played host to the Kansas City Chiefs in an American Football Conference (AFC) divisional play-off game.

It became the longest game ever played in the NFL.

After regulation, the two teams were tied at 24–24. In the first overtime period, neither team could manage to score. A second overtime would be needed. Both teams missed chances to win, as first Kansas City and then Miami missed field-goal attempts.

Finally, with 8:20 remaining in the second overtime, Miami's Garo Yepremian made a 37-yard (33-m) field goal to win the game, which lasted 82 minutes and 40 seconds.

The Giants pounce on a Colts fumble during that legendary 1958 championship game.

Giants fullback Mel Triplett struggles to a touchdown from the 1-yard line in the second half.

15-yard (14-m) touchdown pass to give the Giants their first lead at 17–14. As the skies grew darker above the stadium lights and the winter temperature dipped lower, the Colts turned to their leader for another miracle.

Today's football teams routinely practice their two-minute drills so they can use those final moments of a game to make a key score. Teams put in special plays or special sets, change their signals, and often work without a huddle. All of these innovations were inspired by Unitas, the cool, steely-eyed quarterback who practically invented the two-minute drill.

He worked his magic in this game, too, driving the Colts 86 yards (79 m) with less than two minutes to play. With seven seconds left on the clock, Baltimore kicker Steve Myrha made a 20-yard (18-m) field goal.

Sudden-Death Overtime

Fans were stunned. The score was tied, 17–17, but there was no time left. For the first time ever, sudden-death overtime would decide the NFL championship. The first team to score any points would win. The fans watching at home knew they were seeing an NFL first, too. For them, it would be but the first of many NFL games they would enjoy on TV.

Giants receiver Frank Gifford—later of network broadcast fame—scored a touchdown in the fourth quarter of the 1958 NFL championship game. He also contributed two fumbles early in the game; however, both turned into scoring opportunities for Baltimore.

The overtime started with the Colts holding the Giants on the first series of downs. Then the Colts took possession of the ball, and Unitas did again what he did best, driving his team relentlessly downfield. Hitting his receivers with pinpoint precision, Unitas led his team to the 1-yard line. As the Giants fans screamed for their team to hold off the Colts, and millions of people around the nation sat on the edge of their seats, Unitas handed off the ball to running back Alan "The Horse" Ameche.

Ameche bulled his way in, and when he fell in the end zone, the game was over! Colts fans ran onto the field, the players lay on the ground exhausted, and TV viewers witnessed history.

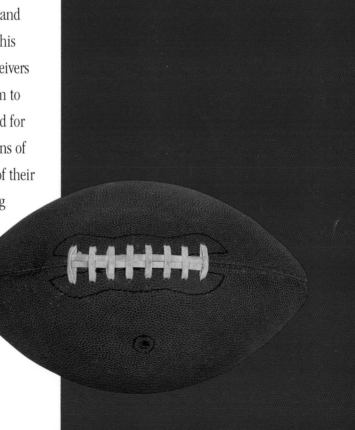

THE ICE BOWL

The Packers and the Cowboys Battle in Subzero Temperatures

The fans' frozen breath creates a sea of steam over the 1967 "Ice Bowl" in Green Bay.

Mustaches froze. Toes turned purple. Fans were bundled up in the stands like Eskimos. The referees couldn't use their whistles, so they just yelled. In the team band, a trumpet player's horn froze to his lips. Movie cameras on the sidelines stopped working. And yet, the game went on.

The morning of December 31, 1967, dawned clear but icy cold in Green Bay,

Wisconsin, home of the fabled Packers, who had won the last two NFL championships. At Lambeau Field that afternoon, the Packers would play host to the Dallas Cowboys in the NFL championship game, with the winner advancing to Super Bowl II in January.

One thing stood in both teams' way: the weather.

Subzero Situation

The temperature was 13 degrees below zero (−25 degrees C). The icy breeze made the wind-chill index read 48 degrees below zero (−44 degrees C). Only a day before, it had been more than 30 degrees warmer. But overnight the temperature had dropped to subzero. Human beings were in danger of freezing just being out in the cold, let alone trying to play a football game on the frozen turf.

But nothing stops a football game, not even these horrible conditions. More than 50,000 fans packed the stadium, while the players got ready to play the game that would always be remembered as the "Ice Bowl."

The Packers somehow completed two touchdown passes to take a 14–0 lead. But the Cowboys' defense, known as "Doomsday Defense," was among the best ever in the NFL. They swarmed over Packers quarterback Bart Starr, sacking him eight times. After recovering a pair of fumbles from frozen Packers' hands, the Cowboys closed the gap to 14–10.

In the fourth quarter, as players and fans were nearing their breaking point in the icy conditions, the Cowboys used a trick play to take the lead for the first time. Dallas running back Dan Reeves took a handoff and rolled to his right, but instead of running, he threw an option pass. Downfield, Lance Rentzel was all alone and caught the pass to complete a 50-yard (46-m) touchdown.

Green Bay quarterback Bart Starr withstood a tough Dallas defense, as well as frostbite, to lead his team to victory over the Cowboys.

Green Bay took over with less than five minutes to play and nearly 70 yards (64 m) of ice-cold, rock-hard ground to cover. Using runs and short passes, Starr led his team to the Dallas 1-yard line with only thirteen seconds left. Starr trudged to the sidelines to consult with Coach Vince Lombardi. The future Hall-of-Fame quarterback was cold, he was tired, and he could barely hold the ball. (To this day, Starr has a tingle in his fingers from frostbite.) But he knew what he had to do.

"Let me take it in," he told the coach.

The Final Play

At third down, and only those thirteen seconds left, the Packers and Cowboys summoned the last reserves of their strength and lined up. Both teams struggled for a foothold, trying to dig into the icy dirt. The ball was snapped to Starr's bare hands, and guard Jerry Kramer opened up a small hole in the Dallas line.

"I found a little divot in the dirt for my left foot," Kramer said. "It was like I had a starting block."

Starr clutched the ball as tightly as he could, followed Kramer's block, and fell into the end zone. Touchdown! The Packers had overcome the weather and the Cowboys to emerge once again as champions.

"It was the worst day ever for football," said Green Bay's Hall-of-Fame linebacker, Ray Nitschke. "And the best day for football."

NFL fans agreed. In a 1999 poll, they named it the "most memorable NFL game ever."

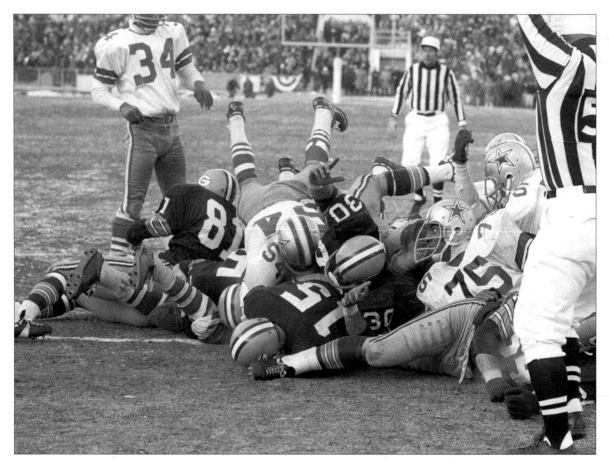

Bart Starr plunging across the goal line to score the Pack's winning touchdown. The hard-fought win earned Green Bay the NFL championship—and a ticket to sunny Miami, where they defeated the AFL's Oakland Raiders in Super Bowl II.

THE LOMBARDI LEGEND

Leading the Packers in the Ice Bowl was the most famous football coach of all time, Vince Lombardi.

He got his start in football as a top college lineman, one of Fordham's "Seven Blocks of Granite." He became an NFL assistant coach in the 1950s and took over the Packers in 1959. Using a toughness that was second to none, and allowing nothing to get in the way of winning, he molded the Packers into one of football's greatest dynasties. The team won five NFL titles in seven seasons between 1961 and 1968, including the first two Super Bowls.

"Winning isn't the most important thing," he was supposed to have said. "It's the only thing."

"Coach Lombardi treated us all the same," said Hall-of-Fame lineman Henry Jordan. "Like dogs."

How tough was Lombardi? At the Ice Bowl, he supervised his team's pre-game practice wearing only a short-sleeved shirt!

Lombardi died of cancer in 1970. In his honor, the huge silver football-on-a-pedestal award given to the Super Bowl champions is now called the Lombardi Trophy.

"I GUARANTEE IT!"

Joe Namath Stuns the World

You've probably heard the story of David and Goliath, how little David knocked off the enormous Goliath using only a slingshot.

Now imagine if David had gone into that fight boasting that he would win, even going so far as to "guarantee" that he'd defeat the giant.

Joe Namath was pro football's version of that second kind of David.

Heading to Super Bowl III

In 1969, the New York Jets were champions of the American Football League, but that league was considered second best to the older and more powerful National Football League. In fact, the two leagues were in the process of merging under the

In 1969, New York Jets quarterback Joe Namath put himself, his team, and the fledgling American Football League on the line by "guaranteeing" a win in Super Bowl III over the Baltimore Colts of the mighty National Football League.

NFL banner. The annual Super Bowl had become a test of "which league is better," and in the first two Super Bowls, the Packers of the NFL had won easily.

Heading into Super Bowl III, no one thought the Jets would do any better against the NFL-champion Baltimore Colts. The Colts had lost only one game all season, while winning fifteen, and pounded Cleveland 34–0 in the play-offs to reach the Super Bowl. Fans and writers who paid attention to the oddsmakers believed that the Colts would defeat the Jets by more than seventeen points. The team was so sure it would win that its owner had already hired a band to play at the victory party after the game.

But none of that bothered Joe Namath. During the week before the Jets and Colts would meet in the Orange Bowl stadium in Miami, the outspoken young Jets quarterback stood up at a banquet and answered a question this way: "Are we going to win? Yes, we are. I guarantee it."

Namath's boast was something that was just not done in the pro football. Talking like that was like waving a red flag in front of a bull,

Namath, as cool, composed, and confident as ever in his trademark white shoes, sets himself to pass against the Colts' defense.

Joe Namath calling signals during Super Bowl III.

or in this case, in front of forty or so enormous Colts. Baltimore was steamed, and they planned to make Namath eat his words.

If anyone could make those words stand up, it was Namath. The brash young passer from Alabama was in only his third season, but he was already regarded among the league's best, famed as much for his white shoes, high-profile lifestyle, and long sideburns as his amazingly quick release.

A Victory for the Underdogs

Early in Super Bowl III, Baltimore did its best to help Namath, not hurt him, dropping several key passes, including one sure touchdown, and throwing three interceptions. New York, meanwhile, was crisp and efficient all day long, as Namath mixed passes and runs well, keeping Baltimore off balance. Matt Snell scored on a 4-yard (3.6-m) run, and Jim Turner kicked three field goals to give the Jets an improbable 16–0 lead in the fourth quarter.

NFL fans couldn't believe what they were seeing. The upstart team from the AFL was beating the veteran NFL squad.

The Colts called on legendary passer Johnny Unitas, whose career was nearing an end, to come off the bench, but he could lead them to only one touchdown before time ran out. The Jets had pulled off perhaps the greatest upset in in pro football history, knocking off Baltimore 16–7.

The Jets' victory instantly elevated the AFL to equal status with the NFL and would soon make the merger between the two leagues smooth and solid. Many experts consider this championship contest the most important game in modern NFL history because of its lasting impact off the field.

Back on the field, as Namath ran toward the exit, he waved his index finger in the air.

"Number one," it symbolized. "We're number one!" And the AFL's David headed to the locker room to celebrate with his teammates.

Super Bowl III MVP Joe Namath, his usual talkative self, was more than happy to meet with reporters following the Jets' stunning upset over Baltimore.

OTHER GREAT NFL UPSETS

- **1950:** Cleveland 35, Philadelphia 10. The Browns, another team from a rival league (the All-American Football Conference), enter the NFL and stomp on the defending champion Eagles.
- **1975:** Dallas 17, Minnesota 14. A last-play, 50-yard "Hail Mary" touchdown pass allows the underdog Cowboys to defeat the 12–2 Vikings in a playoff game.
- **1995:** Carolina 13, San Francisco 7. In their first season in the NFL, the expansion Carolina Panthers defeat the defending Super Bowl champion 49ers.
- **2002:** Super Bowl XXXVI was supposed to be a mismatch. With a regular-season record of 11–5, the New England Patriots weren't even supposed to win the AFC championship, let alone the Super Bowl. With their NFL-leading 14–2 regular-season record, the NFC-champion St. Louis Rams came into the game as heavy favorites. Most fans figured it would be over by halftime. But the Patriots put on a stellar defensive show and shut down the Rams for most of the game. Coming back from a 17–3 deficit, St. Louis scored two touchdowns to tie the game at 17–17 and, to most people's thinking, set the stage for a showdown in overtime. To top off the excitement, however, young quarterback Tom Brady led New England downfield with less than two minutes to go in regulation time. Brady's inspired drive set up the only championship-winning field goal in NFL history, with a mere seven seconds left to play, a 48-yard (44-m) kick by Adam Vinatieri that split the uprights. Final score: 20–17. The underdog Patriots were suddenly the surprise NFL champs!

THE IMMACULATE RECEPTION

The Steelers Produce an Amazing Play

You could forgive the Pittsburgh Steelers' fans for not quite knowing how to act when they headed to Three Rivers Stadium on December 23, 1972, for an AFC play-off game. After all, their team hadn't made it to the play-offs since 1947 . . . and they had lost that game.

From 1933 to 1971, the Steelers were consistently one of the worst franchises in the

Pittsburgh Steelers quarterback Terry Bradshaw produced a miracle play that helped propel his team into the 1972 AFC championship game and put the Steelers back on the map as one of the NFL's powerhouse franchises in the 1970s.

NFL. Their owner, Art Rooney, had won the money to buy the team by betting on horse racing, and he had become one of the most beloved owners in the sport. But his teams just couldn't seem to win. The way things were going, thought Steelers fans, it would take a miracle.

On that chilly day in 1972, they got one.

Taking on the Raiders

The Steelers had reached the play-offs with a group of young players just coming into their own. Quarterback Terry Bradshaw had finally become the starter after being a first-round draft pick three years earlier. Rookie running back Franco Harris was among the best young players in the league. On defense, the "Steel Curtain" was being built, as players like "Mean" Joe Greene, Jack Ham, and Mel Blount were turning into what would become one of the greatest defenses of all time.

Facing the Steelers were the Oakland Raiders, one of the best teams from the old AFL and a team also filled with stars.

The Steel Curtain did its job for most of the day, holding the Raiders scoreless and knocking out starting quarterback Daryle Lamonica, while the Steelers' offense generated a pair of field goals. Then, late in the game,

Pittsburgh running back Franco Harris gaining a few yards for the Steelers in their 1972 AFC play-off game against the Oakland Raiders.

backup quarterback Kenny Stabler scored for Oakland on a 30-yard (27 m) run, giving Oakland a 7–6 lead and making Steelers fans think, "Here we go again. . . ."

The Miracle Touchdown

But then the miracle happened. With twenty-two seconds left, Bradshaw dropped back to pass from his 40-yard line. He was aiming at running back Frenchy Fuqua, but the ball, Fuqua, and Raiders corner-back Jack Tatum met at the same instant.

The football bounced off of, well, someone, and flew back toward the line of scrimmage. Harris saw the ball and, in one of the most celebrated catches in NFL history, snagged the football with his fingertips just inches above the turf. On a dead run, Harris headed for the end zone and made it untouched. No one knew what to think. Was it a touchdown?

Art Rooney, the popular owner of the Pittsburgh Steelers, inspired both affection and loyalty from his players.

NFL rules at the time said that if an offensive player tipped the ball, another offensive player couldn't catch it. Officials ruled that the ball had come off of Oakland's Tatum, thus making Harris's catch legal. When they finally signaled touchdown, Three Rivers erupted in cheers and noise.

Riding in an elevator down to the locker room at that instant was Art Rooney. "What happened?" he asked the elevator operator.

"I don't know," the man said. "I think we won!"

Pittsburgh had won, thanks to a catch known forever as the Immaculate Reception. It was the springboard to the Steelers winning four Super Bowl titles in the next decade.

To this day, when asked whether he touched the ball, Fuqua just puts on a big smile and says, "We won the game, didn't we?"

HELMET TRIVIA

Want to impress your friends with some great NFL trivia? Ask them if they know what NFL team has a logo on only one side of its helmets. Then ask them what that logo is called.

They probably won't know.

The Steelers have logos on only the right side of their helmets. When they first got the logos, the story goes, the equipment manager didn't like them too much, so he put them on just one side to see how they looked. Tradition took over from there—once worn that way, the team never changed.

The logo itself is made up of three shapes that look a bit like squished squares in a formation called a "hypocycloid." The three shapes represent not only Pittsburgh's three rivers, but also the elements vital to the steel industry that is the largest business in town. The three shapes are colored yellow for coal, blue for steel, and orange for iron ore.

"THE PLAY"

College Football's Comeback Miracle

What do you call an event that involves rugby, a marching band, a trombone, and an axe?

In Berkeley, California, they call it simply "the Play."

Each November for nearly a hundred years, the University of California at Berkeley ("Cal") and Stanford University meet in a football contest known as the Big Game. The two schools are bitter rivals. Both are among the nation's elite universities, but both rarely have top-notch football teams. But no matter what the teams' records are, the Big Game is always the biggest game each team plays each year.

John Elway, shown here in his playing days at Stanford, is regarded as one of the best college quarterbacks ever.

In 1982, Stanford boasted one of the best college quarterbacks ever— John Elway, a rifle-armed senior who would go on to lead the Denver Broncos for sixteen seasons and win two Super Bowls. He wanted nothing more in 1982 than to end his Stanford career with a win in the Big Game. Also, a win would give Stanford a shot at a postseason bowl game.

Cal was not bowl bound, but it wanted to end Elway's college career and keep Stanford from a bowl game. And it wanted the Axe.

Playing for the Axe

The Axe is a red, white, and gold axe head mounted on a solid wood plaque; the winner of the Big Game gets possession of this trophy for a year.

Late in the game, which was played at Berkeley's Memorial Stadium, with a beautiful view of San Francisco Bay, Elway seemed to have made his wish come true. Using his amazing scrambling ability, he had led Stanford downfield where they would score what seemed to be a go-ahead field goal, giving his team a 20–19 lead with only four seconds left. As the ball sailed through the uprights, the Stanford team rushed onto the field to celebrate, joined by the unruly Stanford band. The field goal counted, but Stanford still had to kick off to Cal, and now the referee had handed Stanford what would turn out to be a crucial 15-yard (14-m) penalty for their premature celebration.

Four seconds were left, time for one more play.

It's important to note here that Cal had one of the best rugby programs in the nation, winning nearly every National Collegiate Athletic Association (NCAA) title, and that several Cal football players had rugby experience. In rugby, you can only pass the ball backward. In football, that's called a "lateral."

As Cal's team lined up to get the kick, which would come way back from Stanford's 25-yard line due to the penalty, they urged each other, "Don't fall with the ball." They didn't.

A Crazy Kickoff Return

The kickoff bounced crazily downfield, where it was grabbed by Cal's Kevin Moen. As Stanford tacklers approached, he rifled a lateral across the field to Richard Rodgers. Rodgers flipped the ball backward to Dwight Garner. Surrounded by red jerseys and falling to the ground, Garner flipped the ball back to Richard Rodgers, who grabbed it and headed downfield.

Ahead of him he saw Stanford players— but he also saw the Stanford band! Thinking Garner was down, the band once again had rushed the field to celebrate, as had some other Stanford players. Rodgers lateraled to teammate Mariet Ford, who sprinted forward another 15 yards (13.7 m). As he was hit at about the 20-yard line, he blindly flung the ball backward.

Miraculously trailing the play was Moen, who had caught the kickoff to start this wild ride. He grabbed the ball from the air and took off running, dodging tuba players and Stanford's "tree" mascot. He reached the end zone, where he landed unceremoniously on a trombone player, bending the instrument and completing the single wildest play in football history.

Cal's fans now stormed the field to celebrate. Stanford players walked around, stunned. At the center of a mass of people, the seven officials huddled. "Did you blow a whistle?" they asked each other. "Any penalties?" The answer in

A crazy kickoff bounce and a remarkable series of lateral and backward passes lead to an improbable sprint toward the end zone by Cal's Kevin Moen against arch-rival Stanford. Here, as the Stanford marching band scatters in disarray after twice in a matter of minutes having rushed onto the field before play had ended, Moen crashes through the goal line and scores the winning touchdown in the 1982 "Big Game."

both cases was no, and when the referee's arms went up above the crowd, seventy thousand Cal fans screamed as one. The five-lateral touchdown counted, and Cal had won the Big Game, 25–20.

To this day, Stanford lists the game in its record books as a 20–19

Following his impressive college stint at Stanford, John Elway went on to a sixteen-year career with the Denver Broncos.

victory, on the theory that Garner was actually down and the touchdown shouldn't have counted. But in the real record books— the ones that count—the Play is permanently recorded in sports history as giving Cal its stunning win.

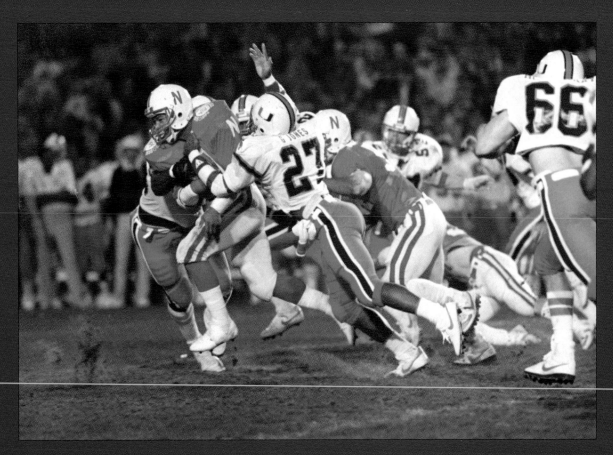

ANOTHER LAST-SECOND VICTORY

Many important college games have been decided on unusual final plays. In 1984, the unofficial national championship was decided that way.

In the Orange Bowl, Nebraska faced Miami, a hometown favorite. The Nebraska Cornhuskers came in ranked number one, but they were trailing for much of the game. With forty-eight seconds remaining, Jeff Smith ran in for a touchdown that tightened the score to 31–30, Miami. An easy extra point would have tied the game and probably given Nebraska the national title, but Nebraska's coach, Tom Osborne, chose to attempt a two-point conversion, which would have won the game.

It was a gutsy call. There was no overtime in college football at that time, so the game could have ended in a tie, but the national championship probably would have been disputed.

Nebraska quarterback Turner Gill rolled out to his right and flipped the ball toward the end zone. But Miami defensive back Ken Calhoun barely got a hand on the ball and knocked it down. Osborne's gamble had failed. The ball went back to Miami, the game ended just a few plays later, and Miami had won both the Orange Bowl and the national championship.

MIRACLE IN MIAMI

The Little Quarterback That Could

Every kid who was ever a football fan has dreamed of being the quarterback of a favorite team. In that dream, it's the big game, and you have time for one last play, one last chance to win the game with a miracle pass. Your best friend is the wide receiver. You take the snap, fade back, and throw it—as far and as long as you can—and your best friend catches the ball in the end zone for the game-winning touchdown!

Guess what happened in 1984 to a little boy turned college senior named Doug Flutie?

That dream came true.

Flutie was the quarterback for Boston College (BC). At 5 feet, 9 inches (175 centimeters), he was too short, many people said, to play quarterback for a major college. But Flutie had led Boston College to its best season in decades. Still, he and his fellow Eagles—including his best friend, wide receiver Gerard Phelan—needed a miracle to end their great season with a victory.

In 1984, quarterback Doug Flutie led Boston College to one of its best football seasons ever.

That Dream Day

On November 23, 1984, the day after Thanksgiving, BC was playing Miami, the defending national champions. The big, bad Hurricanes had made mincemeat out of most of their opponents that season, and there was no indication the Cinderella boys from Boston College would fare any better.

The game played out nearly as expected. While Boston College fought hard, Miami appeared to have the game won when they scored a late touchdown to forge a 45–41 lead. All that was left, it seemed, was for the Hurricanes to run out the clock and send their fans home from the Orange Bowl happy once again.

But Doug Flutie was not done playing. He gathered his team around him and confidently told them if they got to midfield, they'd have a chance. With seventy thousand people screaming for Miami to hold, Flutie somehow led his team to the Miami 48-yard line with six seconds to play.

Time for one last play. For one last, long pass. For one "Hail Mary," as football players call these last-ditch efforts.

Flutie took the snap and faded back. The Miami defense swarmed over the line, trying furiously to sack the elusive little passer and end the game. Flutie escaped their grasp, but they chased him all the way back to his own

Celebrating their win over Miami, Flutie (right) hugged his teammate and best friend, Gerard Phelan, who caught Flutie's stunning Hail Mary pass.

37-yard line, 15 yards (14 m) behind the line of scrimmage.

Flutie knew he had one chance and that he had to throw the ball with all his might. He did just that, the ball flying through the air as if it had been shot out of a cannon. It spiraled

baby. All the Miami defenders could do was watch in disbelief as Phelan was hoisted atop his teammates' shoulders. Flutie sprinted down the field to join the celebration and leaped into Phelan's arms as the two roommates celebrated the winning touchdown.

The Heisman Trophy, awarded each year to the best player in college football, went to Doug Flutie in 1984, the year he and his teammates performed their "Miracle in Miami."

Calling the Play

Here is how fans around the nation watching on TV heard the play described:

Well, here's your ballgame, folks, as Flutie takes the snap, he drops straight back, has some time . . . Now he scrambles away from one hit . . . Looks . . . Uncorks

through the night, through the glare of the Orange Bowl lights, all the way toward the far end zone, 63 yards (58 m) away. There stood Phelan, other BC receivers, and a handful of desperate Miami defenders.

Down came the ball—over the outstretched arms of the Miami defenders—and into Phelan's arms! The ball hit Phelan between the numbers, and he fell backward in the end zone, clutching the football to his chest like a

a deep one toward the end zone. Phelan is down there . . . OH HE GOT IT! Did he get it? HE GOT IT! TOUCHDOWN! TOUCHDOWN! TOUCHDOWN! BOSTON COLLEGE! HE DID IT! FLUTIE DID IT. HE GOT PHELAN IN THE END ZONE. TOUCHDOWN! IT'S ALL OVER!

For the millions of people who saw the play and heard these words, it was a sight and a sound they will never forget. For college football fans everywhere, it is a moment that is frozen in time—little Doug Flutie throwing the ball 63 yards (58 m) for the winning touchdown against the defending national champion Miami Hurricanes.

The Miracle in Miami, as the play became known, clinched the Heisman Trophy for Doug Flutie, honoring him as the best college player of the year.

The memory of this miracle play lives with Flutie to this day.

"Every time I see that play," he says, "it still brings a smile to my face."

THE COMEBACK KID

Even after Doug Flutie's famous touchdown pass in Miami, many people still thought he was too small to be a legend. Initially, he was not much of a success in the NFL, with many coaches still believing that his size was too much of a liability in pro football.

He proved them wrong in the Canadian Football League, where he didn't just succeed—he starred. Flutie became the most celebrated player the league has ever known, winning its Most Outstanding Player award a record six times.

In 1998, he finally returned to the NFL, where his inventive plays, his scrambling feet, and his desire to win overcame worries about his size. He led the Buffalo Bills to the play-offs with a series of come-from-behind wins that reminded many of his college days.

In 2001, he joined the poorly performing San Diego Chargers as their starting quarterback. Flutie has come a long way from that Miracle in Miami, but teams today still look to him to come to their rescue.

SAN FRANCISCO'S SUPER SAVE

Joe Montana Creates a Fantastic Finish

Joe Montana led the San Francisco 49ers to some amazing victories, including some of the greatest comebacks in NFL history. In fact, in a 1984 game against New Orleans, Montana brought the 49ers back from a 28–0 second-half deficit to win 31–28. It is still the greatest regular-season comeback ever.

What made Montana so good? He had an average arm, he wasn't very fast, and he wasn't very big. He just had a quality of leader-

San Francisco 49ers quarterback Joe Montana looking to hand off to running back Roger Craig against the Cincinnati Bengals in Super Bowl XXIII.

ship, of commitment, of confidence that he could get the job done, no matter what. That attitude spilled over into the huddle, making the 49ers a team that owed their success and power as much to their minds as to their bodies.

Facing the Bengals

In 1989, Montana got a chance to work his magic once again. For most of Super Bowl XXIII, the 49ers were having their way with the Cincinnati Bengals, driving repeatedly into Bengals territory. But although the 49ers ended the day outgaining the Bengals 453 yards (414 m) to 229 (209 m), with just over three minutes left, the Bengals took a surprising 16–13 lead.

Montana gathered his team while the coaches devised a plan for the last drive down the field. The 49ers had 92 yards (84 m) to go in less than three minutes.

"Okay, guys," Montana said calmly, "here we go."

The Last Drive

Smoothly, methodically, Montana led his team downfield. He attempted nine passes and completed eight of them, and the only miss was on purpose when he saw that his receiver was too well covered. But perhaps more than his near-perfect passing, Montana's teammates were amazed at his cool under fire. At one point, while the entire sports world waited for his next move, Montana turned to his

THE CATCH

Eight years before Super Bowl XXIII, the 49ers and Montana had put together another incredible game-winning play still known today as "the Catch."

Trailing the Cowboys 27–21 in the National Football Conference (NFC) championship game, the 49ers faced a third down from the 6-yard line with less than a minute remaining. Montana rolled out, but the Cowboys stampeded through the San Francisco line.

"I didn't see anything but [Dallas defensive end] Too Tall Jones," Montana said. But he lofted the ball toward the end zone anyway.

Racing along the back line was receiver Dwight Clark, who was not known for his leaping ability. But somehow, when he and his team most needed him, he rose higher than he ever had, snagged the ball with his fingertips, and landed in the end zone for a game-winning touchdown.

Joe Montana calling the play with Jerry Rice in motion during Super Bowl XXIII.

teammates and pointed out a famous actor sitting in the front row. "Hey, guys, check it out! That's John Candy!"

Montana's teammates thought he was crazy. But then they realized he was just trying to spread his calm throughout the team. They all laughed, and the tension was broken. The march went on.

With just more than a half-minute left, the 49ers reached the Bengals' 10-yard line. Montana called time-out and discussed the play with head coach Bill Walsh. They decided on a pass play aimed at running back Roger Craig, but Montana had a backup plan if Craig was covered.

At the snap, Montana quickly saw that Craig was indeed blanketed by a Bengals defender, so he went to his second option. Spotting wide receiver John Taylor angling in from the left side, Montana zipped a pass between two Cincinnati defenders and hit Taylor in stride right between the numbers.

Touchdown, San Francisco—and with it a Super Bowl championship, the third of four that Montana and the 49ers would win. With everyone in the stadium on pins and needles, Montana had played this last drive like he was taking a walk in the park.

"When you're a kid playing in your backyard, you always win the Super Bowl on the last play," Montana said. "To have that come true for me, well, that was fun."

It was also one of the most exciting moments in Super Bowl history.

San Francisco wide receiver John Taylor hauls down a catch as Cincinnati defensive back Ray Horton moves in for the tackle.

BIG BOWLS OF RICE

Wide receiver Jerry Rice of San Francisco was named the Most Valuable Player of Super Bowl XXIII. In that game, he caught eleven passes for a Super Bowl–record 215 yards (197 m). Rice also holds virtually every important NFL scoring and receiving record. Here are his key totals, each an all-time record, through the 2000 NFL season.

Career receptions: 1,281

Career receiving touchdowns: 176

Career total touchdowns: 187

Career receiving yards: 19,247 (17,592 m)

Consecutive games with at least one catch: 209

Single-season receiving touchdowns: 22

Single-season receiving yards: 1,848 (1,689 m)

FOOTBALL'S GREATEST COMEBACK

The Bills Fight Back from a Thirty-two-Point Deficit

Losing 28–3 at halftime of an AFC play-off game on January 3, 1993, the Buffalo Bills could have easily thrown in the towel. No one thought they could come back and defeat the Houston Oilers. In fact, in the locker room at halftime, Coach Marv Levy simply asked them to try their hardest.

The Bills hadn't expected to be in this position at all. They had had a terrific 1992

Frank Reich, backup quarterback for the Buffalo Bills, orchestrated a stunning come-from-behind win over the Houston Oilers in an AFC play-off game in January 1993.

regular season leading up to this game. They had won the AFC championship the season before, and in 1992 they had tied for the conference's best record at 11–5. Their "no-huddle" offense, led by quarterback Jim Kelly, was a scoring machine. They had one problem in this game, however—Kelly was injured and didn't play. Without him, the offense sputtered.

A Second-Half Sensation

Buffalo backup quarterback Frank Reich had not been able to do much against the Oilers, while Houston had had its way with the Bills. At halftime, the home team trailed by twenty-five points. The all-time record at the time for comebacks was twenty-eight points, so the situation looked hopeless.

It got worse early in the second half when the Oilers' Bubba

Wide receiver Andre Reed teamed up with Frank Reich to score three touchdowns in the second half of the Bills' 1993 AFC matchup against the Oilers.

McDowell returned an interception thrown by Reich for a touchdown and a 35–3 Houston lead. Fans started heading for the exits, and TV viewers hit the remote control. Turns out they missed a heck of a show.

About six minutes into the third quarter, Buffalo scored to make it 35–10. Levy called for an onside kick, rarely used this early in a game. "But what have we got to lose?" he thought. Buffalo kicker Steve Christie recovered it, and Reich hit Don Beebe with a touchdown pass soon after.

35–17.

A few minutes later, after forcing a Houston punt, Reich threw a touchdown pass to Andre Reed, the Bills' Pro Bowl wide receiver.

35–24.

Fans who had left tried to scale fences to get back in, while others in the Buffalo area ran to their radios and TVs to join in the fun. Near the end of the third quarter, Reich and Reed teamed up again for a score.

35–31.

The fans who had stayed to watch the

Veteran Oilers quarterback Warren Moon tried to fend off Buffalo's comeback drive, but his efforts were thwarted by an overtime interception and a Houston penalty.

38–35.

Houston was reeling. The players couldn't believe what was happening to them. But the wild comebacks weren't over yet. Houston's Warren Moon guided his team on a final drive into Buffalo territory. With just seconds left in regulation, Houston's Al Del Greco nailed a field goal that tied the game and sent it into overtime.

Breaking the Tie

Fans, players, and coaches were drained. The second half was fast and furious and filled with scoring, great plays, and the biggest comeback in NFL history. And overtime was still to be played? What else would these two teams come up with?

The drama ended quickly, however. Moon's first pass was intercepted by Buffalo cornerback Nate Odomes, who returned it inside

game were going nuts while the Oilers tried to stop the steamroller. They couldn't. With just over three minutes left in the game, Reich and Reed hooked up for another score that, amazingly, gave the come-from-behind Bills the lead for the first time in the game.

Houston territory. After only two plays and a 15-yard (14-m) face-mask penalty against Houston, Buffalo kicker Steve Christie made a 32-yard (29-m) field goal to complete the greatest comeback victory in NFL history.

41–38, Buffalo.

In a game they could not afford to lose, the Bills had staged the greatest comeback in NFL history, rallying from thirty-two points down to victory. They would go on to play in the second of their four consecutive Super Bowls less than a month later. The Bills couldn't come back in that next game though, and they lost the Super Bowl to Dallas by a score of 52–17.

Above: *Buffalo's quarterback Frank Reich (14) and kicker Steve Christie celebrate the Bills' unbelievable 41–38 play-off victory against Houston—a win that Christie nailed down with his 32-yard field goal in overtime.*

"I'VE BEEN HERE BEFORE"

Bills quarterback Frank Reich must have felt oddly comfortable in the second half of that great Buffalo comeback. Amazingly, Reich also led the team that set the record for the greatest comeback in college football.

In 1984, Reich's Maryland team was behind 31–0 to a powerful Miami team. But he rallied the Terrapins (that's another name for a turtle) to a stunning 42–40 victory.

A TRULY SUPER TACKLE

The Rams' Defense Saves the Day

Coming into Super Bowl XXXIV, most fans thought that offense would be the main show. The pass-happy St. Louis Rams had put on a remarkable display in the regular 1999–2000 season, setting several NFL scoring records under the leadership of their strong-armed quarterback Kurt Warner, the NFL's most valuable player.

Opposing the Rams on that January 2000 day would be the Tennessee Titans, a team that depended on

Tennessee Titans quarterback Steve McNair gamely scrambles for yardage against St. Louis defenders Kevin Carter and Grant Wistrom in Super Bowl XXXIV.

running and strong defense. The Titans had been the Houston Oilers until 1997, when they moved to Memphis, Tennessee. In 1999, they moved to Nashville and became the Titans.

Taking on the Titans

In the first half, the Rams outgained the Titans in yards, 294 (269 m) to 89 (81 m). They moved the ball almost at will, advancing inside the Titans' 20-yard line six times. But Tennessee stiffened up in the red zone and had allowed the Rams only nine points on three field goals.

The Rams finally scored a touchdown early in the second half, with Warner hitting Torry Holt to give St. Louis a 16–0 lead.

Then suddenly, the Titans' offense came to life. Taking advantage of the bull-like running of Eddie George and the scrambling passing of Steve McNair, the Titans scored twice to cut the Rams' lead to 16–13. Then, with just over two minutes remaining, the Titans made a 43-yard (39 m) field goal that tied the game.

The Rams' lightning-strike offense quickly struck back, as Warner lofted a long, high pass that Isaac Bruce ran under and caught. Eluding two Titans tacklers, Bruce streamed into the end zone for the go-ahead score.

Two-Minute Warning

But at 23–16, the biggest play of the game was yet to come. McNair led a two-minute drill to perfection, using short passes, runs by George,

STUCK IN A HOLE

While seventy-two thousand people in the Georgia Dome watched "the Tackle" unfold on the field in front of them, where were more than four hundred members of the press who would describe the scene to the world?

Stuck in a tunnel outside the teams' locker rooms, watching on TV like the rest of the world. I know—I was one of those writers.

With a few minutes left in the game, many writers and reporters headed down to the locker room to interview the players after the game. The walk down took several minutes, so many of us left early to scamper down ramp after ramp to reach the field, many stories below the press box.

Crammed into a low-ceilinged hallway, we watched on TV monitors, stunned, as the Titans marched toward the game-deciding play. All we could think was, if Dyson scores, we have to walk all the way back up to watch overtime!

But Jones made the tackle, and we rushed in to hear the players' stories and then tell the world what they said.

feet, but McNair somehow hopped over him, put down a hand to get his balance, then rifled a 16-yard (15-m) completion to the Rams' 10-yard line.

There was time for one more play to try to tie the game. As the fans in Atlanta's Georgia Dome went nuts watching this intense Super Bowl drama, McNair calmly zipped a pass to a speeding Kevin Dyson at the 5-yard line. It looked like Dyson would make it into the end zone, but Rams line-backer Mike Jones took three quick steps to his right and dove at Dyson's legs.

Jones made a textbook-perfect wrap-

Tennessee running back Eddie George dives into the end zone for a touchdown in the dramatic 2000 Super Bowl contest between the Titans and the St. Louis Rams.

and time-outs. Facing a long third down with time running out, McNair dropped back to pass and was chased by two Rams. One dove at his around tackle, stopping Dyson just inches from the game-tying score. As the two players lay on the turf, the gun sounded, the game ended, and

After Mike Jones's game-ending tackle, Tennessee's Kevin Dyson belatedly tries to "scootch" the ball across the goal line as time runs out on the Titans' hopes for a game-tying TD.

Rams quarterback and MVP Kurt Warner enjoying the post-game celebration at Super Bowl XXXIV.

confetti swirled in the air above the victorious Rams. Dyson lay for a few moments on the ground, knowing how close he had come. "The Tackle," as Jones's super effort is now known, proved to be one of the most dramatic endings in Super Bowl history.

ROOKIE WINNER

Super Bowl XXXIV wasn't the only Super Bowl to come down to the end. A few have ended with a winning—or missed—field goal. One dramatic championship game was Super Bowl V in 1971, a pretty sloppy game, with the Baltimore Colts and Miami Dolphins combining for six fumbles and six interceptions. The two teams were tied at 13–13 with five seconds left to play.

The Colts had the ball, with time for a 32-yard (29-m) field goal that would win the game. Baltimore's kicker was Jim O'Brien, a tall rookie who also played wide receiver and whose long hair stuck out from the back of his helmet as he lined up for the kick.

How nervous was the young player about to attempt the biggest kick of his life? O'Brien reached down to pull up some grass to toss in the air to gauge the wind direction. One problem—the game was played on artificial turf!

But O'Brien nailed the kick and the Colts had only to stop the Miami kickoff return to celebrate their only Super Bowl championship.

Football Time Line

1869   The first college football game is played, between Rutgers and Princeton, using rules that somewhat resemble those of modern football.

1876   Walter Camp helps develop the first code of rules for American football.

1897   In Allegheny, Pennsylvania, the first fully professional football club is formed.

1906   The forward pass is legalized. Prior to this, players could not throw the ball forward but could lateral it backward to a teammate.

1912   Points for a touchdown are finally set at six; a field goal had been set at three points in 1909.

1920   The American Professional Football Association is formed in Canton, Ohio. In 1922, the organization changes its name to the National Football League.

1923   The Rose Bowl is built. It's the first major stadium in the western United States and makes college football a national game.

1933   The first NFL championship game is held. Prior to this, league champions were the team with the best overall record.

1957   The University of Oklahoma completes a record streak of forty-seven consecutive victories.

1958   The sudden-death overtime NFL championship game is seen by millions on TV, helping vault the NFL to the top of the sports world.

1960s   Western powers such as the University of Southern California (USC) journey to the South with integrated teams. Their success and national pressure finally integrates major Southern powers such as Alabama.

1967   The first Super Bowl is played, with Green Bay of the NFL defeating Kansas City of the AFL.

1970   The AFL and NFL merge to form one league under the NFL banner, consisting of the American Football Conference and National Football Conference.

1973   The Miami Dolphins win Super Bowl VII against the Washington Redskins by a score of 14–7, completing a 17–0 season, the only undefeated season in NFL history.

1980   The Pittsburgh Steelers win their fourth Super Bowl in six seasons and become the first team with four Super Bowl wins.

1990   The San Francisco 49ers match the Steelers' record with a 55–10 victory over the Denver Broncos in Super Bowl XXIV. They also win XXIX for a total of five Super Bowl titles.

1995   The Bowl Championship Series is instituted, creating a college system that brings a number-one and number-two team to a single national championship game.

1996   The Dallas Cowboys win their fifth Super Bowl with a 27–17 victory over the Pittsburgh Steelers in Super Bowl XXX.

2002   The New England Patriots pull off a surprise 20–17 victory over the St. Louis Rams in Super Bowl XXXVI.

To Learn More

BOOKS

Buckley, James, Jr. *America's Greatest Game.* New York: Hyperion, 1998.

Buckley, James, Jr. *Play Football!* New York: DK Publishing, 2002.

Christopher, Matt. *Great Moments in Football History.* Boston: Little, Brown, 1998.

Italia, Bob. *100 Unforgettable Moments in Pro Football.* Edina, Minn.: Abdo & Daughters, 1998.

Stewart, Mark. *Football: A History of the Gridiron Game.* Danbury, Conn.: Franklin Watts, 1999.

Tuttle, Dennis. *The Composite Guide to Football.* Broomall, Pa.: Chelsea House, 1998.

INTERNET SITES

ESPN Classic
www.espn.com/classic
Contains biographies of Jim Thorpe, Joe Montana, Joe Namath, and Jerry Rice among many other great football heroes and other athletes.

The Heisman Trophy
www.heismantrophymemorial.com
To read all about the careers of Doug Flutie and other Heisman Trophy winners.

Jim Thorpe Association
www.jimthorpeassoc.com
Information about Thorpe and the Jim Thorpe Award, given annually to college football's top defensive back.

National Football League
www.nfl.com
Official site of the National Football League with links to all the teams' official sites.

Play Football
www.playfootball.com
The NFL's official site for kids.

Super Bowl
www.superbowl.com
Stories of all the great Super Bowls.

Index

ABOUT THE AUTHOR

James Buckley Jr. has written more than twenty sports books for young people on baseball, football, hockey, soccer, and the Olympics. He was an editor with Sports Illustrated *and the National Football League, where he helped start and wrote for nfl.com, superbowl.com, and Play Football, the NFL's official Web site for kids. He is the editorial director of the Shoreline Publishing Group, a book producer and editorial services company in Santa Barbara, California.*